# JOURNAL ENTRIES

Poems

Thomas Grissom

# JOURNAL ENTRIES
### Poems

SANTA FE

© 2011 by Thomas Grissom.
All Rights Reserved.

No part of this book may be reproduced in any form or by any electronic or mechanical means including information storage and retrieval systems without permission in writing from the publisher, except by a reviewer who may quote brief passages in a review.

Sunstone books may be purchased for educational, business, or sales promotional use. For information please write: Special Markets Department, Sunstone Press, P.O. Box 2321, Santa Fe, New Mexico 87504-2321.

Book and Cover design ∼ Vicki Ahl
Body typeface ∼ CG Times and CG Omega
Printed on acid free paper

Library of Congress Cataloging-in-Publication Data

Grissom, Thomas, 1940-
  Journal entries : poems / by Thomas Grissom.
    p. cm.
  ISBN 978-0-86534-818-9 (pbk. : alk. paper)
  I. Title.
  PS3607.R577J68 2011
  811'.6--dc22
                                          2011017685

WWW.SUNSTONEPRESS.COM
SUNSTONE PRESS / POST OFFICE BOX 2321 / SANTA FE, NM 87504-2321 /USA
(505) 988-4418 / ORDERS ONLY (800) 243-5644 / FAX (505) 988-1025

For Becky,
Who makes it all worthwhile

# Contents

### I. This Disembodied Voice

Seattle, Sept '86 — 15
8/86 — 16
If at All — 17
This Disembodied Voice — 18
Lament — 19
A Parable — 20
The Unaesthetic Truth — 21
Paltry Wages — 22
5/19/86 — 23
To String a Few Words Together — 24
5/25/86 — 25
Alice Walker — 26
June 1 — 27
The Clearing — 28
The Hemlock — 29
Scene — 30
6/1/86 — 31
6/8/86 — 32
The Natural Historian — 33
Pathways — 34
December '86 — 35
Acknowledgement — 36
Requiem — 37
The Convoy — 38
Memorial Day — 39
"Forth" of July — 40
10/87 — 41
7/4 — 42
Lessons — 43
Nocturne — 44
William Carlos Williams — 45

## II. A New Beginning

Journal Entry — 49
Working — 51
A New Beginning — 52
Ghost Dancers — 54
Expect Small Differences — 56
The Delta — 58
A Memory to Last a Lifetime — 64
7/88 — 65
Mounds — 66
Scene — 67
Moral — 68
C. Pissaro, 1886 — 70
Manet's Bar at the Follies-Bergere — 72
Impressionism — 74
Charon: Friday Harbor — 75
The Scream — 76
A Lighted Candle — 78
Montana Monster — 80
Montana: Summer '88 — 82
Self-Portrait: Van Gogh — 84
Anniversary '88 — 85
Ditty — 86
wOrDs — 87
Lament — 88
A Change of Mood — 89
Why the Rage? — 90
Prostate — 92
AIDS, 7/89 — 93

## III. A Change of Mood

Sad Songs and Waltzes Aren't Selling This Year — 99
Love in the Age of the Automobile — 100
Long and Short — 101
Crooked and Straight — 102
Explain a Pea — 103

Two Rainbows — 104
E'nuff Said — 105
Notes for a Poem — 106
God Never Sleeps — 107
Vast As the World — 108
There Is Poetry — 109
Poetry Suits Me Fine — 110
I'm Not That Tired Yet — 111
Can Only Put It into Poems — 112
There's Going to Be Another Book of Poems — 113
The Kestrel — 115
Stick Horses — 117
Taking Their Measure — 119
The People Knew — 120
Why Is That? — 121
I Want to Work — 122
Memorandum, 12/89 — 123
Written in Stone — 124
A Truth to Cling to — 125
Saddam Hussein — 126
Chance — 127
The Sailboats — 128
The Loon — 129
Rain — 130
Eyes — 131
Robert Service — 132
O, I Was Born to Wander — 133
Sumas '90 — 134
North of 50 — 135
Near Chetwynd: — 136
Signs — 137
Alaska Highway — 138
Seaside Dawn — 139
Poem '91 — 140
Sappho's Song — 141

Out my window
Six towhees in one tree,
Each one a "Prince of Darkness,"
But not scratching sparrow-like in the underbrush
But perched high up in the hazel
Beneath the towering firs,
Busy with the experience of life—
I thought at once of you.

# I. This Disembodied Voice

## Seattle, Sept '86

Through the cobbled streets
up a hill from
Pike Place Market, past
alcoves along the
alley, there
scrawled on the wall
in the blaring spray-paint
sounds of silence:

Poetry Lives—

The city blinks and
whispers its answer,
in the bustle and noise of crowds,
the distant scream
of sirens...

## 8/86

Searing,
As though on hot pavement,
Spilling your guts
At their feet
For all the world to see,
Flinching—
Not from pain
But fear,
That someone will know
It is your guts,
Or worse—
That they won't.

## If at All

It isn't simple.
It is all very complicated. Nothing
ever changes that, no degree of understanding
or sophistication, the green hills and
barren deserts by which we stumbled our way
here bleeding and unabsolved, burdened
with images: recalled later they explain
nothing, fit no algorithm, give rise to
no principle, and can only be expressed
in words unredeeming; we
store them up one by one then struggle
to write these lines that some one or two
may say what was meant, uncertain
what it is, or if anyone can ever
know. Nothing ever changes that—
no amount of time or reason,
no experience or wisdom: whatever
we know, we know unknowingly,
if at all.

## This Disembodied Voice

I can speak to them
But not face them,
Look straight into their eyes
From afar, here
Inside myself, where
No light shines but my own
And one moves freely
In shadows; in words
Echoing in my ears
Shameless and unrestrained
That which is really me,
Not this false veneer
Politeness wears; from
This refuge I speak to them
Freely, not hearing or needing
Their reply, it does not
Change the truth
But only slows its pace;
Those who know me will
Not know my words,
Those they touch would
Loath accept me as their
Author; from here
I speak in words
Untempered by concern,
But never deem to face them,
As of no consequence
Or purpose
To this disembodied voice.

## Lament

I have been too long away
From where harsh words will have their say,
In sounds grown sweeter by the measure;
If I come not there another way,
Perhaps in night grown bright as day,
Those others all the more a treasure.

## A Parable

A single voice and new,
Coaxed halting from the shadows
Of its solitude, and sounding
Still its desolation, drew
From all those others
That had gone before
In ways it never knew,
And never could restore.

## The Unaesthetic Truth

Like all things real they were
Flawed, here and there ink stains
On the pages that I bartered
For their praise and money. Later,
When the harsh words had smitten,
They cursed me for my candor
And charged me with dishonesty,
Pointing to the unaesthetic truth.

## Paltry Wages

One verse
Then two
The first one pink
The next one blue,
Then joy is streaked
By tears in time
The cadence clumsy
Strained the rhyme,
As sorrow yields
To grief and worse
The stanzas lengthen
Verse by verse,
Till what is earned
Is truth itself—
A stingy, biting
Penurious wealth.

## 5/19/86

*The moving finger writes and having writ*
*moves on...*

Those old words no longer work,
And these new ones are not enough
Now to say what I mean;
Can it be they never were,
That what I took for truth
Was just something that I felt
But never did express? Why then
Would your eyes betray you
So, your smile, the sweet embrace—
Is not a truth once found
Ours to claim forever?

## To String a Few Words Together

I just want to string a few words
Together, he said, string them together
In such a way to say some things
That keep on welling up inside me,
Needing to be said; perhaps to say it
In a way that will mean something
To someone else, to tell them I
Was here too, that I understood,
Because without it life is not enough;
But mostly just for me, he said,
Just to string a few words together.

## 5/25/86

Days and nights of endless striving—
All this
And more will still be here
Long after I am gone—
Growing older is but to grasp
That one essential truth;
Why then confront inexhaustible folly
With words
And such a puny fury?
Because we shall not be here
And must have the answer sooner.

**Alice Walker accused Faulkner of racism, but I thought it only a lover's quarrel and wrote this reconciliation:**

>She was
>black
>but actually
>a rich warm
>brown
>not fawn
>but not too dark
>either
>not at all
>like the shiny black
>that sometimes
>resembles
>the color purple;
>and he
>white
>and
>aristocratic
>with a mustache
>and
>sad eyes;
>what they
>shared
>was just
>their anguish
>and
>the eloquence
>that spoke its
>pain;
>it
>would be hard
>to know
>which
>was more alike.

## June 1

Morning light and a
cool freshness mingle
outside my window,
beyond the reach of
fir and hemlock;
Rejoicing finches
herald the vibrance
of a new day, with
its infinite (count
them) possibilities.

## The Clearing

This world here begins where
That other one ends, there
At the edge of the clearing
Along the neatly gardened border
Separating lawn and woods—
On this side all is ordered and
Carefully arranged, the grass mowed
And flowers weeded; the other side
Is all darkness and mystery
Behind hemlock and elderberry,
What lies hidden in fern and bracken
We have grown to fear,
And deny its cunning as our own.
For centuries we have cleared
These spaces in the forests
To fill them with our idols—
They will outlast us but a little.

## The Hemlock

It stood
Squarely at the forest edge
Between darkness
And that brighter impulse that
Bared the land about its feet,

The day bright ants were seen
To scale its heights
In thickening streams,
Beneath a rain of browning needles;

Concerned, she gauged which way
It might come down when next
The sea wind moaned—too much rain
Makes roots take shallow hold—and
Measured yard and house in the prospect;

Not that way—against the wind—he said,
Nor the opposite, crashing through the forest wall,
But there, somewhere in between,
Along a line of least resistance
Between opposing forces,

The way it grew,
Not so much to find the light
As just to escape the darkness, he said,
The way all things are wont to do.

## Scene

Screeching inconsolably
outside my
window

an angry jay
curses
the woodlot cat

intent upon a meal
of eggs and featherless
young

who even now
the tip of its tail
slowly flicking

meticulously
places
each footfall

not to rustle
a single
leaf.

## 6/1/86

In the dark they caterwaul
And cavort outside my window,
And soon there will be more cats
To eat the birds nesting
In these woods and in the hedgerows
Turning green and full of spring;
It has been this way forever, that
Innocence should succumb to mystery
And evil comprise its own innocence,
And hopefully it will always be,
Forever is but that span
Which we can know; still
There is something sinister
In this, these killers we keep
And coddle that they may creep
Forth at night, half wild
Half tame, risking nothing
Not even an empty belly
On the chance of failure;
No matter—they have cast
Their lot with ours, and ours
Is what it's always been,
Theirs no better in the trade.

## 6/8/86

The cattle lying
peacefully
in the grass
below the hill,
viewed picturesquely,
are in reality
feeding flies and ticks
and mosquitoes;
so too
are we each
consumed
by this insatiable maw.

## The Natural Historian
### (To R. S.)

A twinkle in the eye
Conceals a mind
Too flinty
For such soft deception;
The bees dance to a tune
Unknown, Arachne's
Tapestry tells no truths,
Merely observe—
The intricate steps, each
Silken strand—
No answers, but questions
Their patterns reveal,
Save one:
This the only truth.

## Pathways

Among the many from
Which to choose, freeing
And opening outward, there
Are pathways restricting
And confining, some
Dead-ended, others endless
Yet leading nowhere;
The choices it seems
Are by no means equal,
The paths now stretching
Before us connected
To those that brought us here.

## December '86

*The philosophers said nothing—*
*The poets have said it all...*


Mouth all the unscreamed agonies of the ages,
Dream the disappointed dreams,
Think all the tormented thoughts, those too
Born of anguish and despair where
No hope is, we would not have it otherwise—
All else is dullness and stultifying:
We shall likely just murder ourselves in the end
To keep from dying of our boredom.

## Acknowledgement

Too long distorted and coerced,
this mind
does not fit that mold:
rationality
violated by absurdity—
some of us
are meant to live as aliens,
discovering it
later
rather than sooner.

## Requiem

These Greeks turned it back upon
        itself,
Made the gods too mortal and
        killed them:
Anthropomorphic death—
Replacing them instead with this
        stingy materialism
From which we have yet to recover,
Bent upon following their reason
        lean and hungry
Like a wolf on the slopes of Mt. Ida
To wherever its prey seeks refuge.
They were right you know—
        only
Man cannot live this way.

## The Convoy

Distinct
against the autumn
haze it crawls
segmented
like a many-legged
dragon through the
riotous countryside,
the feet Europe
the serpentine head
Vietnam
the great camouflaged body
Grenada
Managua
or Havana—
here where there
is no war,
where there is only
the fading warmth
of the equinox
and the first faint promise
of winter,
the creatures of war
crawl about
and make ready.

## Memorial Day

An honor guard of citizens
Marshaled on the bridge and threw
Bright garlands on the placid waters below,
Brass-tipped the pinioned shafts that thrust
Their flags unfurled against the breeze;
A cannon shot rang out—
The passing cars all slowed to watch—
Stern words recalled the deeds of honored dead;
And in reflections mirrored there
I imagined that I could see
Images of a future foretold,
What our fate will likely be.

## "Forth" of July

O lofty Pericles, gifted orator
Where art thou
At the hour of our greatest need
Who spoke
In polished phrases like gleaming marble
The golden lies
That made men yet awhile
Want to strive
And sacrifice for Athens. These modern lies
They speak
Like rough-hewn stone are only base
And foolish
From which to cringe in shame,
Yet serve
As well for these Athenians. Your
Flowery speech
Was wasted Pericles, less noble words
Will do—
The result, I fear, the same.

## 10/87

You do not wish for me
to look back on this
with the same fondness
it gave rise to—Why should
any find contentment if you
do not? This is to be a peace
purchased at the price of pain,
these the ties that bind
and hinder. Broken, there
will be a breach forever.

## 7/4

When I see them
      together
            in the stores

and shopping malls
      at breakfast in restaurants
            the mismatched couples

time mocks
      in sullen silence
            some difference

in age or color
      or other of the measures
            by which we judge

unkindly
      coping with crowds
            and little annoyances

I wonder—
      are they any longer
            kind

to one another?

**Lessons**

Your mouth was pretty,
pursed in pouty protestation,
and as we talked I
wanted it on me, to
feel its smooth wet warmth
pressing soft against me
looking deep into your eyes,
while I explained
whatever it was you
didn't understand; there
are so many other things
than these, I thought,
you could better explain
to me.

## Nocturne

I love you

I love you too
she said and

sealed it with a
kiss in the dark

more lovely
than any light

they would ever know.

## William Carlos Williams

The awkward
little poems
he wrote
in strangely
broken lines
kept running
broken through
my thoughts
to suddenly
join together
un broken
just the
way he
had intended.

# II. A New Beginning

## Journal Entry

I was finally able to work.
I feel much better about it.
Do you know what I mean?
At least there is something to report.
*Was it good?*
Yes.
Of course.
I was able to work again.
In that sense it was different.
I was able to finish something.
For a while, I was able to work.
A beginning, perhaps.
Yes.
A beginning.
*But was it good?*
Yes.
Perhaps.
I think so.
It is still difficult to be certain.
But perhaps.
*Was it like before?*
Yes.
In some ways, yes.
Yes, but also no.
*In what ways?*

No longer having to deny something that is important
—no, necessary—
but which you are afraid you won't be able to do again
And not having to also deny the fear and the doubt
and live with the uncertainty,
And knowing that no matter what, you did it as well
as you know how
And that for now you couldn't do it any better
And that is all that counts.
*Yes?*
And the feeling of wanting to again
Of wanting to because it is important, because it is the
most important thing there is
And nothing else matters as much
Or in quite the same way.
*Yes?*
*And did you like it?*
Yes.
Oh, yes.
I liked it.
I liked it very much.

## Working

Where do you get this stuff, he asked,
I mean where does it come from;
How do you think of it?

It comes from within, he said,
And I don't think of it—
It's just there—and when I sit down
To work it comes out, sometimes slowly and
Painfully, sometimes in torrents,
And sometimes not at all.

But however it comes out, he continued,
That's the way it is, just
The way it's meant to be;
And all I know is that when it works
I like doing it more than anything,
And when it doesn't—well,
I always have to try again.

## A New Beginning

Click
Click
Click
Tap  Tap  Tap
What purpose does it serve?
What purpose could there be?
Not straightway but
Oblique*ly*
To strike some new direction
(That is, to swerve)
Cast off with renewed verve
Yes.
No, nerve.
(Get the juices flowing)
You take yourself too serious*ly*
Yes the trees grow very straight here
They grow tall and very great here
Sunset and dawn come late here
And there are thrushes everywhere
But Capt Jack
Was a poor Modoc
He lies now on his back
And Chief Joseph's words won't sound
(No more forever)
That eloquence he once found
And spoke on prairie wind

He lies now on his back
The children lie there too
And Crazy Horse alone was right
He understood they had to fight
Still thrushes sing more sweetly
Than do finches
Than do sparrows
Though swallows are the greatest fliers
(Three miles out on the road today
Next time maybe more)
What purpose does it serve?
What purpose could there be?
Not straightway but
Oblique*ly*
To strike some new direction
You take yourself too serious*ly*
And these things are only found within
Just the way it's always been.

## Ghost Dancers

What should you have expected
O smiling children of the Northwest—
That there would not have been these
        bullet holes
Nor the crimson stains in the dirty snow?
That the soldiers would not have pursued
Joseph's valiant band relentlessly,
To the borders of the Land of Winding Waters,
        Wallowa,
And beyond? That the women and children
        and old men
Would not have died upon the frozen earth,
Joseph thinking himself safe at last
By the "Old Lady's Skirts," and their bodies
        lie bent and stiff
In grotesque mockery of life? That those
Escaping death would not linger saddened
        beyond recovery
To die years afterward, wasted, spirit-broken?
Why should it have been any different with you
Than with the Powhatan and Narragansett
        in the East,
Than with the Iroquois, Miami and Shawnee;
Or the Cherokee and Choctaw in the South?
Why any different for you than for
The Sioux and Cheyenne and Arapaho;
Or the Navaho and Apache in the Southwest?
And with all those too numerous to recall

Who once lived free beyond the rising and setting suns,
From where Joseph now pledges before his people
To fight no more forever, the names
Little Big Horn, Sand Creek and Wounded Knee
Singing mournfully in the prairie winds.
Ghosts now haunt these hills—
They can be felt and seen long afterwards
In the crude monuments that cover over these
Graves and rise to dot the plains,
In the farms and factories, the sprawling cities
      and highways
That mark the passage of power and the new
      progress—
The ghosts of every great clash of wills—
And who can say that it is not right,
That any injustice has been done?
Wowovka and the frenzied ghost dancers
Will not bring back the former spirit,
The imagined greatness; it is an idle dream
That does not disturb the slumber of those
Who fell here to lie frozen in the crimson
      snow; it is best
Forgotten with the false notions of injustice,
O smiling children of the Northwest.
There is no injustice: you have been dealt with
The same: as with all other peoples before you—
Why imagine that it should be any different
      with you?

## Expect Small Differences

The great evils—
Those worthy of this shining we call civilization—
Are with us always:
Straining and labor of the masses
And the people speak, the deed done, some new foulness
Revealed—we recoil in horror,
But mostly later. In this we show ourselves overmatched,
The prescience of the mind outdone by the individual strivings
Of so many bits of sentience all laboring together
Or at cross purposes—we do not know beforehand:
Those crematoria which belched the pall of smoke
And stench of death across a ravaged Europe
Somehow no worse than the gentle fall of raindrops
Laced with acids
To leach away the stain. Hitler again in time
Will have his supporters, Caligula is but an abstraction
Across so many centuries: distance and time cleanse
Everything the same, and who knows
How the future will unfold?
Sometimes it seems that it is either all good, or all evil,
These two great faces we cannot tell apart. In that
There is no solace to deny these words, this torment—
Yet from far enough away it will seem so:

The choking city-haze, the crimson-tinctured sunsets
Will wear both countenances,
The blinding plutonium flash
Signal the start of some new epoch. Caution then,
And calm; treat them both the same: they are twins
Good and evil. Speak of them often
And in the same breath, the same measured tones—
Each equally deserving. Where there is such perfection
Expect small differences.

## The Delta

i)

gray
December
days,
dripping
and bitter cold,
the damp chill
heavy—
with the sweat of slaves
the old Negro told me:
the Delta.

ii)

This land lies buried fallow
beneath
a lifetime of memories,
deeper
than the rich black soil,
richer
and more fallow still.

iii)

To be young
and innocent
in a troubled toil-worn land,

fresh footprints
stamped in the soft soil—
the land wears a new smile
to ward off the old sorrow.

iv)

I crawled up on his lap—
The memory I have
is of the smell of the old Negro,
soft and musty
like soiled cotton flannel,
and of the graying nap on his head—
I ran my youthful hands over it—
You gotta make sump'm o' yo'self
he would tell me,
the tobacco-stained teeth showing through
his smile,
But the cloudy distant eyes held a vacant
faraway look
that told another story.

v)

His old shack burned down one night—
It sat across the street
behind the church—
She saved his life,
they said,
beating on the door to wake him
A pot of water on the stove boiled dry
and melted
He was almost blind.
I never saw him much again after that

He finally got too old
I guess—
I never even thought about him being black,
until later,
or ever did find out
if it mattered to him that I was not.

**vi)**

Sitting cocked on his head the most
unlikely felt fedora with
one hand

he would lift it up scratch the balding
nap with long bony fingers then wipe
his brow and replace it all in one

easy motion the
smooth black face
solemn

framed by a stiff white collar and
sloping shoulders and the tan
gabardine windbreaker

he wore summer and winter un-zippered
at the neck to
reveal a shiny threadbare

tie
fastened at the waist around
the tops of trousers that

reached to shoes too
long unpolished ever
to be again he

looked the part no
ordinary field hand
but

the foreman the only
one who could
bridge

this graying
gap
between black and white.

**vii)**

The face was stern it
had to be
that way but the eyes

compassionate he could say
yessuh without ever revealing
himself the way

he had done
for forty years or more
then relay

the orders on down the
line without being
harsh yet still

stern which was why
he was the
black boss the master's

nigger though the others
never held it against
him he managed

to live just a little
better
because of it.

**viii)**

I love this land
Why? Does
one need

a reason beyond the fact?
besides
I grew up here

I understand its seasons
and
its many moods

its injustices
and hatreds
and bigotry

its tortured cry
of anguish
the dark stains of its past

yet I love it
just the same
can

there be
any
other reason?

**ix)**

I love this land
Somewhere
in the distance

without ever having
to explain
why

a cottonwood
quakes
beneath it

a wild boar
its spine
pierced

with an arrow
three
young savages

kneel
around their
trophy

## A Memory to Last a Lifetime

Two young boys looking for a memory
To last a lifetime see them there
With bows and arrows sleeping bags but
No tent and old pots and pans loading
It all in a cypress johnboat to row across
The lake and enter the wooded bottom
Where wild hogs live two young boys
Looking for a memory to last a lifetime.

## 7/88

Little
word pictures
strokes

of the pen
that capture
images

and sensations
no art
without sensations

the brush strokes
must
convey feeling

the truth
of sensation
is art

whether on canvas
or
on paper.

## Mounds

Each
starts out a
sensation some

idea or
mental image a
bump

on the memory around
which words
are piled

neatly
for the most part
but easily

jumbled if you aren't
too careful
smoothed and

patted into place
who knows
at the outset

which
will make a neat
mound?

**Scene**

White-petaled daisies
twist
on supple

stalks in unison
to stare
yellow-

eyed at the sun
spreading
its white

and yellow carpet
across
the field.

## Moral

A field of daisies
is a fitting subject
for a poem white-petaled

they twist on slender
stalks in unison
to peer

yellow-eyed
at the sun's progress that
alone

is more than adequate
reason or stand head
bowed

in prayerful posture throughout
the night oh and
what about the

occasional maverick
did I mention
in unison who

doesn't follow the
crowd isn't there
a moral

there where so much
is possible little
is accomplished.

## C. Pissaro, 1866

It is a large canvas
a dirt road
along the banks of the Marne

in winter
focuses one's attention to sweep
from the lower left

to the upper right there
the sky lighter
we finally escape the

dark feeling
of the canvas as a whole
and instead

become engulfed in its
luminous tones a woman and
her child

walk the road beside
leafless trees
swallowed up

by the depths of its
richness it is
quite simply

that unmistakable thing
a masterpiece there
are few colors mostly

greens
and grays
and fewer shapes yet

with them the artist
has created a
universe this

is not properly the beginning of
something new
but the

triumph
of all that
is timeless.

## Manet's Bar at the Follies-Bergere

Here facing us
is a young woman her
back

to a mirror the
artist
has taken liberties

with the reflections art
he believed
obeys its own rules yet

we must clearly understand
that it is a
mirror

life
has a depth not
evident

in the flat figure of the young woman
her eyes
vacant

but not unexpressive stare
fixed
straight ahead

masking
what is in her thoughts
for that

we must look much
deeper
in the mirror behind.

## Impressionism

Shadows
have color
whether

Monet or
Pissaro realized it
first

or even Renoir
does not concern us
now it might

almost be taken
as the abstract aesthetic
of impressionism

art
not how we react
to the little

incidents
of our daily lives
though

it would certainly
be appropriate
there too.

## Charon: Friday Harbor

Smiling demurely his
obvious pleasure
signaling

it ever more clearly by
the occasional gesture
and a furious semaphore

of hand signals he
directs the cars onto
the waiting ferry in

the proper sequence
reflecting
some grand design

he has in mind a map
of the voyage each stop
neatly planned

toward
the final destination
how he

relishes it
orchestrating events
in all these lives.

## The Scream

One long, final scream
at the end—

I would have it just so:
Raging and brazen, like
sounding brass, hollow
and anguished, reverberating
down through the ages
filling up the senses

a hundred thousand voices
combining as one

yet not loud,
but as though heard silently
in a dream from which
there is no escape
and no awakening

the last defiant act of outrage
that unites
and binds us together
that accepts, by denying,
what it cannot change
or defy, uttered
in that universal language
there is no mistaking

one last, lingering cry
of rebellion:

I would have it just so.

## A Lighted Candle


She lights a candle
>    where no candle is needed
>>    in the several-hundred-watt glare

of the room
>    which its flame cannot pierce
>>    but its incense can

a candle
>    whose virtue
>>    is its very superfluousness

registered in a flickering symbolism;
Pasternak
>    —said Yevtushenko—

was a candle of conscience
>    not a beacon
>>    the way a small flame

is more noticeable
>    for not dispelling entirely
>>    what gives it form;

this one it seems
>    is to signal
>>    some small protest

of her own
        of modernity itself perhaps
                of the several-hundred-watt glare

and the global combustion
        that lights it too harshly
                dispelling

every shadowed sanctuary
        how to escape it
               in this day

except
        in the simple gesture
                of a lighted candle;

there is a power
        in such small symbols
                what is whispered

is often more significant
        than a thousand shouts;
                better to light a single candle

that way to admire
        the dancing flame
                and acknowledge the darkness too.

## Montana Monster

Pivoted by its tail
it writhes
in great circles

upon the ground
metal spine and truss-work
ribs

held high
on tubular legs rubber-
footed stretch

segmented
across the field
preying-mantis-like

its transparent body of
soft mist glistening
in the sun

anoints with life-
giving elixir all
it touches

here the last great
monsters left their
bones

and footprints fossilized
in dry creek beds
and barren

rock who
will find the footprints
and skeletons

of these monsters
or know
what created them?

## Montana: Summer '88

The trick is the free association
of ideas: thinking like a river—
one ceaseless steady stream
of consciousness, slow and torpid
or swift and turbulent, nothing
too clearly connected, each idea
separately unpredictable
like a brown trout rising
slowly to some imitation of reality
skating on the glassy surface—
what else is reality but the
empty interval between thoughts?
No poem you have written
before now captures that quality
except one, and it frightened you
in its honesty and its innocence,
like a river—why must we first
mull everything over before daring even
to think it, unless afraid of the water
and the mystery lurking there?
We must learn to read the river,
to search out the secrets
eddying in its backwater:
anyone can fathom the clear pools
with their placidity and depths
or the bright riffles with their
sparkling exuberance—cold refreshing
splashes on the face in summer—

but wisdom swirls in the eddies
and the intricacies of the backwater,
moving unexpectedly at times against
the current—none can be certain how,
even after a lifetime of observing
it remains at its core a mystery
and we forever novices; yet
there is a flow to the river,
challenged by the need for composition:
its channel confined between
banks, it has a headwater
and a mouth, and it flows here
more swiftly, there less so along
its journey: the need for structure,
in words if not in thoughts,
for those who will read and judge
unaware that the only meaning
was the thoughts themselves and
can find no more adequate expression:
to sketch in words the way Monet
might have painted it—swiftly,
deftly, to capture the sensation
of the moment that too long considered
becomes ephemeral or stolid;
and always the river winds and meanders
and continually changes its
course, holding to no certain
direction for too long.

## Self Portrait: Van Gogh

The face goes through a metamorphosis
Canvas after canvas—there are
In all about forty of them, this
One of the last is likewise the best—
As does the palette of colors
And the life itself, the artist
Intent upon confronting his own image:
The piercing eyes stare more intensely, the face
Ever more haggard, charged with emotion;
The red beard casts a gangrenous pall
Over the sallow skin, the colors brighter, more
Shimmering project a feeling of madness apparent
In the features and in the events of his life;
The severed ear is not visible though the impulse
Wielding the shears is evident enough.
Gauguin could not help but be impressed:
The background swirls and dances magically
On the canvas, ominously, as if events
Had gotten out of hand, to feel the soft
Bristles in the sticky oils as the colors
On the rough cloth take shape—this
No commercial art, but the creation of a man
Obsessed with capturing at that instant
In one space all that he had lived for;
Gauguin the charlatan was indeed impressed:
He had looked into the very face of art.

## Anniversary '88

I want to write for you love poems,
Words tender—and gentle phrases
Soft and seductive, laughing and friendly
As the mornings spent in the warm sunshine
Our clothes draped over a chair;
To frame forever those feelings
Which moved us then to love—and live—
Beyond the bounds
Where less bold we had no hope to go:
This love cannot age
And be itself; for it time stands still
Beneath such timeless passion,
Or slowly stamps it with a riper, fuller face
That though true
Can never its changeless nature show;
Then words will chisel out the shape
We knew of passion—
In poems—like marble sculptured moments
Out of time,
That are all we ever need of love,
And life, once lived.

## Ditty

I'll write you a love poem
A ditty or two
I'll keep them that simple
They'll always be true

And put in sweet memories
Of things that we shared
And little reminders
Of how much we cared

And I'll be your lover
And you my best friend
Bound by a love
That never should end

So that when we are older
And the years are unkind
We'll have those sweet verses
To bring back to mind

The vows that we made
When our love was still new
And our love like those poems
Will always stay true.

## wOrDs

There are BIG words
and little words—
words like YOU
and me,
like LOVE
and hate
or GOOD and bad—
I don't know
why this should be,
much less
why it is so.

## Lament

O words
So vast we cannot ever hear them
That go upon the page
Without the bite and sting
They need, of this
Is such prosy poesy made
That I grow weary of it.

## A Change of Mood

The gray beneath the firs
outside my window

the lighter gray (but not
white) of the paper

the gray
familiar marks across the page

have all smothered
with their grayness

the sunshine
by which I had hoped to write.

## Why the Rage?

We watch these tortured die,
Their bodies self-consumed,
So matter-of-factly,
As it seems we must—we
Have no cure—and they
Having indulged the body's lust
For love
Or whatever else their purpose was
Must pay the exacted price.
So why the rage for those who only
Abort? Are not their reasons
Equally complex,
And who has any cure
For that which troubles them?
The lump of fetal tissue sucked
Untimely from the womb
Before its innocence could even begin,
Dwarfed by this monstrous indifference
To all the fresh new graves
Of those who were incomparably more
Than either their guilt or innocence.
The two sides scream the challenge
Of their empty, pointless struggle—
The one would give life
By taking it away, the other
Take it away in order to bestow it—

And watch the while
In curious silence
These tortured others die.

## Prostate

The burning urge
for relief following
my morning coffee

pleasurably indulged
becomes more and more
one of life's

predictable pleasures
the little walnut-
sized gland

at the base of the
bladder
growing unchecked

and all there is
to be done
about it

is enjoy
the simple pleasure
of

slowly
pissing
my life away.

# AIDS, 7/89

I.

In the first instance
there was of course
free love or at least
unfettered (they are
wrong about that) there
being then no cures
but no microbes either

Vengeance is mine
saith the Lord but
European arrogance was
more effective—it was contact
with the New World
that rotted Gauguin's brain

except for where
as now
reason or belief could
constrain erect passions—
about that
there was never any mistaking

then finally there were medicines
(though they had been there

in the bread mold
all along) and no one
had of necessity
to perish though some
still did and do

but now passion prevails
as of course
it always has and
not reason or belief
(there being no cures)
can forestall the
biological conclusion.


## II.

The object has always been

to get as many seeds
into the bellies of as many women

as necessary
to procreate the race

there has always been
some price to pay

those who see it as something else
think only in terms

of possibilities
never getting beyond

that fateful deception
who is to say

that where what is possible
conflicts with necessity

there are any possibilities?

# III. A Change of Mood

## Sad Songs and Waltzes Aren't Selling This Year

"Willie Nelson For President"
and
"Honk If You Love Willie"
read
the bumper stickers on the back
of the pickup paused at the light—
Thought was the mischief in him
as he eased his car alongside,
touched the horn one temperate time
and smiled—
A startled look replaced by bearded scowl
returned the greeting
through a muddy cab-door window,
then at the green, sped away
on angry squealing tires—
Oh dear, she feigned,
you don't suppose he mistook our meaning?
Why we only did what he suggested—
I guess subtlety's lost on loggers and
rednecks, he replied.

## Love in the Age of the Automobile

She goes through life on bald tires
He keeps his emergency flashers on
Side by side they drive life's roads together
She is the constant chance of collision
He directs the traffic for her.

## Long and Short

A bow is long
An arrow is short
A long bow bends
A short arrow stays straight
A short bow doesn't shoot a long arrow long
A long bow shoots a short arrow short
Who is to say where short ends and long begins?
That's the long and the short of it.

## Crooked and Straight

A bow is crooked
An arrow should be straight
A straight bow won't shoot
A crooked arrow won't shoot straight
A bow is held crooked by a straight string
An arrow holds itself straight
A crooked bow shoots a straight arrow straight
This is where straight makes crooked and crooked makes straight.
That's the crooked and the straight of it.

## Explain a Pea

You ever try to explain anything?
Anything at all. Explain a pea.
A pea is not so great. It's
Not as big as a mountain
Or as wide as a forest.
It's not as deep as the ocean
Or as high as the sky.
A pea is just a pea.
But try to explain it sometime.
Where does it come from?
And where does it go?
What does it have to do with anyway?
Faster than you can answer one question
Twenty others spring up to take its place.
You can't ever get finished because
You can't even get started.
See if you can do it. Try it
Sometime. Explain a pea.

## Two Rainbows

Two rainbows side by side
In the same sky
One above the other.
I looked again
And there was only one.
The raindrops splattering on the road
Spelled out:
"No sky deserves such splendor."

## E'nuff Said

You can't write a poem
If you ain't got nothin' to say,
That's the simple truth of it
The plain facts of the matter,
A poem's got to say something
Something worth saying
So much and no more,
Otherwise silence is the best policy
Silence is golden
E'nuff said.

## Notes for a Poem

Their love of adventure is what brought them together
She liked the things he did that she had never done
He admired her zest for life. When they married
They told each other they were embarking on a great adventure
Together they explored the world
Each new experience kept the adventure going
The weeks became months, the months stretched into years
As the years passed they were able to do less and less
Of the things they used to do
The adventures became more modest
Where before they had climbed mountains or escaped in wilderness
Now they strolled in parks or explored some quiet corner
Finally even the minutes dragged slowly by
To them it did not matter.
Each moment became a new adventure.

## God Never Sleeps

Lately I have traveled to the north country
In summer there the forests are never dark
The sun skims along the horizon,
The domed forehead of the sky swings its
Cyclopean eye southward,
Briefly blinks,
Then looks back northward again.
In summer in the north country God never sleeps.

In winter there the forests are always dark
The sun struggles below the horizon
The sleeping giant keeps its drowsy eye shut
Lesser lights blaze and twinkle in the dark
Like images in a dream
Things scurry and scuffle in the frozen silence.
In winter in the north country God never sleeps.

### Vast As the World

It is a small garden
Along one side, twining up a trellis, sweet peas
Bloom in patriotic profusion
In one corner sugar peas shade their succulent pods
Snap beans dangle deep in green
Potatoes burrow beneath brown soil
Broccoli flaunts its furrowed face
Spinach and lettuce twist tight their leaves
About their heads. There a bare spot
Where the squash will not make this year
And here and there a yellowed leaf
Or stalk, fare for the slugs.
Overhead the watchful eye of the sun
Stares down.
It is a small garden
Vast as the world.

**There Is Poetry**

I've been looking for poems in all the wrong places,
In big things, as though the size of subject
Determined the vault of verse—In big events,
And in big ideas, the latter a hazard of
The profession I have followed lately: trading
In ideas, bartering and swapping them for pay
As though they were some kind of currency
And could be bought and sold. Wisdom has it
The best things are free and come in small packages—
Some poet must have thought of that; any worthy
Of the claim knows it for the truth. Size
Is not the measure of the verse. What point
In building up that already too big to grasp?
No, the trick is seeing the bigger that lies hidden
In the small. There is mystery in a smile,
The melodious fluting of a thrush, the silence
Of a stone, and there is poetry too.

## Poetry Suits Me Fine

Being a poet suits me fine.
Mystery is it, certainty's a gag
We play on ourselves and one
Arm twisted up behind your back.
Let the philosophers hunt in circles
Let the scientists search for truth.
What can be explained is not poetry,
Said Yeats, and that's all right by me.
Being a poet suits me fine.

## I'm Not That Tired Yet

This is about those writers who died too soon,
Like brilliant colored flowers that do not last the season,
Those who killed themselves, and those who just got tired
At some point and decided to quit living;
All those writers who believed the struggle was no longer worth it
And gave up on life.

I think about them often, when I read the words
By which they contradicted the final act, yet
I don't judge them; I think I understand
How they felt, and why.

I don't dwell on it.
I read the words again, and know that I'm not like them.
I get a good night's sleep.
I'm not that tired yet.

## Can Only Put It into Poems

I've got no business writing poems
I still don't understand them
Though by now I've written quite a few
(Some one or two I even liked, or convinced myself I did)
But no, I still can't put it into words
Exactly what it is that makes a poem
Even when I get it right
The words all lined up straight and true
And know it for the real McCoy
Can't tell another soul why
It worked this time
Or how to do the same again
Can't put it into words at all,
Can only put it into poems.

## There's Going to Be Another Book of Poems


I had friends
But I disappointed 'em.

Some said I would be a famous scientist,
Some said a doctor or lawyer or executive,
Maybe even a general or politician,
But at any rate someone who would take charge and figure things out,
Someone who would run things, make things happen, get things done.

That's what my friends all thought, or said they did.
But I disappointed 'em.
Others were not so sure—still they believed
I might amount to something, do something important—
But I disappointed them, too.

No one thought a poet
Least of all a rebel and a maverick,
Someone who would thumb his nose at the system
Question the wisdom of it all
And turn his back on it—
Not wanting to take charge and make things happen
      and fix the problems,
Not even convinced anyone could ever understand
      what that is anyway—

But a poet, saying what he thinks, telling the truth
Questioning the wisdom of it all,
Not wanting to say too much, not even here.

I disappointed 'em.
They ask me: What are you going to do?
What I'm doing is what I'm going to do,
I tell 'em.

## The Kestrel

Struck from the skies by what freak
Accident or bird of prey the injured kestrel
Skulks through the scrub willows and rocks
Beside the stream. Undaunted, defiant,
Its bottomless eyes bright and burning,
It eludes its tormentors,
No pain, but the bone-shattered wing
Dragging useless in the dust. Trapped,
It could not escape these, a curious
Crowd of hikers who with glasses
And field guides encircle and hold it
At bay. The patient, staring eyes
Look up, asking nothing, revealing
Nothing, only the fierce intensity
Of the life shining out of them.
Does it recall? realize? regret? Or
Is that fierceness all indifference?
Does it think of the young who will
Perish, the mate searching in vain,
The life slowly ebbing? Its eyes
Give no clues, these things cannot be
Separated from the form huddled
In the scant cover. Those other eyes,
Staring down, reveal all, they are windows
On the mind. Analyzing, regarding,
They search in vain for answers

Where there are only questions,
And miss those deeper questions
Where they see only answers.
Identified, recorded, sex noted,
They prepare to move on,
Leave the injured kestrel
To find refuge for the night
From the jays and the ants,
Let nature take its course—
As though nature were something separate,
As though they could step back
Unthreatened from the fate of the falcon.
It won't survive. These
Others, continuing, will—
Yet only for a while.

## Stick Horses

I remember the yellow stick horse
I rode as a child.
That it was a broom handle
One end worn smooth and polished
By dragging it on the hard-baked ground
Was easily enough forgotten.
It carried an old cotton towel,
Folded, for a saddle,
A rope, threaded
Through a hole and knotted
Served as the bridle
When I rode it at a furious gallop,
Hardly ever less than a brisk trot:
It was a spirited creature
Unaccustomed to walking,
No pony could have been
More real to me.
It was a time of magic and wonder
When a child's unbridled imagination
Creates the only truths he needs,
Or acknowledges, recalling and recapturing
The lost innocence of our species.
Now we are older and wiser—
More sophisticated, we have learned
The ways of the world.
That they are inventions of our

Imaginations, these stories we tell ourselves
About the world
Is easily enough forgotten:
They are spirited creatures
The products of our imagination
And go at a furious gallop,
Unaccustomed to walking;
No truth could be
More real to us.
We have explored the globe,
Walked on the moon,
Tamed the world's wild horses—
But still in our minds
We ride stick horses.

## Taking Their Measure

At times we have had need of strong Presidents.
When we were a young nation there was Jefferson,
And Jackson. And when we were a nation divided
There was Lincoln, whose stubborn vision gave us
Our future. Earlier in this century, when we were
At war, there were others who made a difference,
And afterwards one or two who challenged us, but
Were killed or ignored. Then came the respectability
Of middle age with its stingy prosperity and security,
And the need for great leaders was past. Still,
Of some, it is said they did well by the country—
The truth is otherwise: the country did well by them.

## The People Knew

They are not to be trusted, the leaders on both sides told
               the people.
See the destruction of two wars, the death of millions,
               the fields of gleaming gravestones.
And one side: See the ghettos and the slums, the poverty
               and the prejudice.
And the other: See the loss of freedom, the abuse of human rights.
And both: Their people are enslaved still, and their leaders would
                   conquer the world. We must be strong, arm ourselves,
                   prepare to annihilate the other side.

Now the walls are coming down, the barriers are being dismantled
Brick by brick. The historians, the political scientists, the thinkers,
They do not know why, they did not predict it.
They were all caught unawares.

The people knew.
They told the politicians, the world leaders
On both sides, enough is enough. You are wrong.
We are tired of your way, your arguments make no sense.
You are merely foolish, said the people, we will not follow you.

The leaders were wrong. They thought only of themselves.
They listened to their own arguments and heard only what
They wanted to hear, believed only what they wanted
To believe. The leaders were not to be trusted.
The people knew.

### Why Is That?

Some people hold an idea more real than an acorn.
Why is that?
Out of one can grow a tree, a forest, and a wilderness
       stretching endlessly from sunrise to sunset;
Out of the other can grow an action that levels the forest,
       and raises up in its place farms and settlements
       and great cities and civilizations, and books and music
       and works of art, and the sort of determination
       that men are willing to die for.
Why is that?
One can provide food and shelter and fires for warmth;
The other fuels the fires that make food and shelter
       and warmth not enough.
Why is that?

## I Want to Work

It isn't leisure that I need, but work
Honest labor, spit in each palm and rub them together
Roll up your sleeves and pitch in—
Not escape from the drudgery and demands of a job
But toil, the sweat of one's brow, tired muscles
That know the pleasure of a good night's sleep,
The satisfaction of something worthwhile accomplished;
It's all this leisure that makes me tired.
I've had too much of ideas and books and easy conversations,
Of what-if's and what-might-have-been's—
God speaks through actions, make a choice and get on with it;
You can keep your leisure, I want something to count on:
A job, some task, a chore—
A duty, something to point to with pride:
I want to work.

## Memorandum, 12/89

We will make our annual pilgrimage
To see the birds;
These others will have to swallow
Their disappointment:
More assurance in the one
Than in the other.

## Written in Stone

I love you Patti—
He wrote it high up on the hillside
In stones laid out in long straight rows
Big enough for all to see as they rode
Back and forth to town or went about
Their chores. The stones gleamed white
In the summer sun. In winter
They glistened in the rain and mist.
The cows ate the grass around them
And the woodchucks left them undisturbed.
Years later, they could still be seen,
Long after he had changed his mind.

## A Truth to Cling to

I love you, he said.
He told her he could not live without her.

I love you too, she replied.
Without him, she said her life would have no meaning.
Each knew it was not true;
Yet it was a truth that they could cling to.

Each went their separate ways, and each lived.
And through it all, it was a truth that they could cling to.

## Saddam Hussein

Saddam Hussein—
A name to write beside Hitler
Mussolini, Stalin—
A bully and a butcher, he is in good company
Our century has had so many,
Those known and all those nameless
Who do their bidding, who shout and cheer
And carry out their orders.
They revere him in Baghdad. They have seen the bodies
Bloated in the desert, the young boys and old men
Gassed, their throats burning, the skin sloughing off.
Like all the others before him he is a nobody.
Like them he lacks imagination, no grasp of the human
Capacity for suffering and sacrifice and endurance
That will be his undoing.
History will blot him out too—
Grind him under its collective heel, the empty skull
Bleaching in the burning sands. In the meantime
Many will suffer and die. Someone do them a favor
And slit his throat.

## Chance

Snick, snick, snick, snick, snick,
The impulse sprinkler spurts its jets of water
All about on the thirsty lawn, one spot
Withered and already browning, too many days
Since the last rain. The blades will wilt and die
Against the coming season of soaking rain
When the roots will again send up new shoots
Until the next drought. How does the grass
Know to do this? Natural selection,
The survival of the fittest, tells nothing
Of how it came to be; for that
We revert to chance. It is the chant of
Our century: Whatever we cannot comprehend
We attribute to chance.

## The Sailboats

The sailboats teeter in the wind
They thrust their arms upward
And cup their hands and hold them out to catch the breeze.
Their hulls, hissing, slice through the waves.

The sailboats scurry and weave before the wind
Their sails billow in the breezes
Little rows of silvery bubbles spread out behind.
The hulls make a thin smile
And bow and nod to the waves.

## The Loon

All night long on the lake
Where fog spreads its torn blanket
And waves lick the stony shore
A loon utters its haunting cry
Forlorn and maniacal
As though the spirit of wilderness
Were about on the night
Peering into each cove
Searching every bay.

## Rain

Outside
It is raining
The raindrops falling softly
Against my window
Running in little rivulets
Down the pane

Inside
The day is gray
The teardrops falling softly
Against my face
Running in little rivulets
Down my cheek.

## Eyes

Eyes, eyes
Everywhere
The silent, staring eyes
Eyes that see the past vacant
Eyes that see the future featureless
Eyes that see but have lost their sight
See them everywhere
The cold, indifferent eyes.

See the bright and cheerful eyes
Eyes full of hope
Eyes that see the past unflinching
Eyes that see the future unafraid
Eyes that see with vision clear and certain
See them flashing
The brave, undaunted eyes.

## Robert Service

When I read this simple verse of his
My head goes round and round
As in and out march images
To a cadence of measured sounds,
In a few tight lines he tells a story
Tells it straight and true
Of how he cremated Sam McGee
Or the death of Dan McGrew,
Of nights alone and books unread
And things for which he had no time
So that he might toil instead
To capture thoughts in verse and rhyme,
That I might sit and sip my sherry
And in one or two such lines
Find some truth for the worn and weary
To repay him for his time.

## O, I Was Born to Wander

I was born to wander
Can't sit too long in one place
But what boredom creeps into my soul—
My God, I'm fifty
There likely isn't that much left
To me of time
When I waste it sitting still I get nervous
Just thinking of departing
With regrets for all those things undone
Places never seen
Can't sit too long before I'm worried
I'm wasting too much of me
In one spot
The books grow dull, the thoughts all the same,
I need to see some new possibilities—
The one time I tried it, put down roots for awhile
I soured on the world;
Some folks say the birds migrate
To escape the cold and starvation,
But I know it's only wanderlust
And to seek some brand new options:
O, I can't sit too long in one place
I was born to wander.

## Sumas '90

At the border
they wanted only
to know
where we were from,
how long
we planned to stay,
and whether
we were bringing gifts

that was all—

nothing else;
nothing
that told them
who we were,
or anything about us
really—

## North of 50

Climbing the Fraser River
Canyon
hot
and dusty
through forests of thirsty Ponderosa,
on the slopes
chamisa and sage—

What of those
haunting tales now—
about the numbing cold
and a frozen
north land

## Near Chetwynd:

A columned, porticoed
manor
like some Southern
mansion
presiding over plantations of
aspen and alder

A newly plowed field
ahead of it twelve
frost-free
weeks
in back of it
fifty million
acres of wilderness

In the driveway
a sign:
        Free Kittens

## Signs

East of Whitehorse:
    POSTED
    NO HUNTING

North of Yellowknife:
    FOR SALE

## Alaska Highway

It took a war
to open up this country;
it would take another one,
or a loss of spirit,
to ever close it.

A history of man
on earth
is a history
of roads.

## Seaside Dawn

This thin, lone cry
traveling down the dwindling night
will usher in a dawn
still and dripping,
the shrouded sun
wrapped in fog, and
muted promise of what
for the several seasons
allotted no one
I have spent the hours
shirking, till now
the smooth, worn tires
on the wet sand
leave tracks more distinct:
the patient water
seeps back in and
washes them away again;
though, for all that,
the beach years later
is not the same.

## Poem '91

The words
that only I know the meaning of
elliptical, oblique, but not obscure—
not the words themselves, but what they mean for God's sake—
arranged
in some order thought out by me,
again
not because anyone else will understand
but because for some strange reason that's
the way I thought they should be

whatever it is I thought will
not come through, merely
broken fragments like those of Sappho or Catullus
or someone else who lived too long ago
to matter anymore, even
if I had gotten it right
would it
have made any difference?
would they have known
anyway?

## Sappho's Song

Object of
my affections

Aphrodite's favorite

Every moment
you are in my thoughts;
I am *devote*d
to you

I *dote* on you

How can I say it
more simply?

www.ingramcontent.com/pod-product-compliance
Lightning Source LLC
Chambersburg PA
CBHW031137090426
42738CB00008B/1117